CORE COLLECTION

Core Collection

Poems about eating disorders
by
SARAH SIMON

Adelaide Books
New York / Lisbon
2019

CORE COLLECTION
Poems about eating disorders
By Sarah Simon

Copyright © by Sarah Simon
Cover design © 2019 Adelaide Books

Published by Adelaide Books, New York / Lisbon
adelaidebooks.org

Editor-in-Chief
Stevan V. Nikolic

All rights reserved. No part of this book may be reproduced in any manner whatsoever without written permission from the author except in the case of brief quotations embodied in critical articles and reviews.

For any information, please address Adelaide Books
at info@adelaidebooks.org
or write to:
Adelaide Books
244 Fifth Ave. Suite D27
New York, NY, 10001

ISBN-10: 1-950437-50-7
ISBN-13: 978-1-950437-50-4

Printed in the United States of America

this collection is dedicated to anyone who finds that a poem, a line, a word — feels dedicated to them.

Contents
(& discontents; cheers to you, Sigmund Freud)

note from the author	**11**
i am not quite a latte,	**13**

Δ

The First Line I Took From Nina Simone	**17**
Choose Your Fate	**18**
Reluctant Scientist	**20**
Halloween Poem	**23**
Famine In The Family	**24**
Excuses Become Muses	**31**
Drink Your Milk	**32**

Equations, No Art.	*36*
House Of Limbs Not Liturgies	*38*
How Beautiful It Is To Be Hungry –	*42*
Que Bello Es Tener Hambre,	*43*

ΔΔ

Decisions Diamond To Observers	*47*
Our Bodies Are The Unspoken Agreements	*50*
What To Do With Tendencies Hold	*51*
Aspire	*54*
Wind Necessitates Tempestuous	*55*
Vv (Fangs; I'm Hungry)	*56*
Raw	*57*
Collarbone	*58*
You Can't Eat Desserts Forever	*60*
Vacuum Diet (On Binge Eating)	*62*
For Two Months, Every Meal Fostered A Fear Of Babies	*63*
Sex Symbols	*64*

CORE COLLECTION

ΔΔΔ

Going Under	*71*
C i n g u l u m	*76*
Waking Up From A Dream And Into Smoke	*80*
The Peculiar Pain Of Examining A Map	*84*
How To Read A Map	*85*
Core	*86*
Daré A Luz A Una Soledad	*88*
I Will Give To Light, Birth, To A Soledad	*88*
Dis –	*99*
Más Que Yo	*102*
Woosh!	*104*
Always Mention The Nuts	*105*
Boiling Water	*106*
Crumb (A La Mamacita)	*108*
La Mujer Como Yema	*111*
Woman As Yolk	*113*
List of credits	*117*
About the author	*119*

note from the author

it wasn't until the sister of a friend asked to interview me about my eating disorder. she was working on a project for grad school, tampering with the idea that eating disorders should be understood as existing along a spectrum, much like schizophrenia and autism currently are. now, this is not to say that these disorders are even remotely related – just that they share a nature. i do not doubt that every disorder in the DSM will eventually be looked at by the medical community in this way.

to finish the thought, it wasn't until then that i recognized common threads in much of my poetry, all knotting back to my eating disorder: food, exercise, a fascination with bones, body feeling, anxiety, depression, emptiness, a fear of being full. maybe you can point out some others for me, further helping me reach the subconscious of the subconscious that is supposed to be poetry.

p.s.
if you want to know why i seem to like triangles so much, ask me

I AM NOT QUITE A LATTE,

but rather a cappuccino
who thinks she just wants a plain ol'
Joe, no sugar –
no milk –
no foam –

but she is not just a plain ol' Jane;

it is the perfection of shape
that she seeks, a fantastic form.
a body that she thinks
milk cannot support,
as in her bones, she becomes
weak;

yes, for lack of calcium,
but yet too many
bananas, her "safe food," plenty of
potassium;

until when, at the first sip of an accidentally-ordered
– not-asked-for –
cappuccino,
sitting outside in the
sunshine

with Diego,
enamorado –
she sips it anyway,
for being *three whole dollars*.
and then, after all the hours spent sipping
muddy waters,
she decided to cut the bitterness
with fat

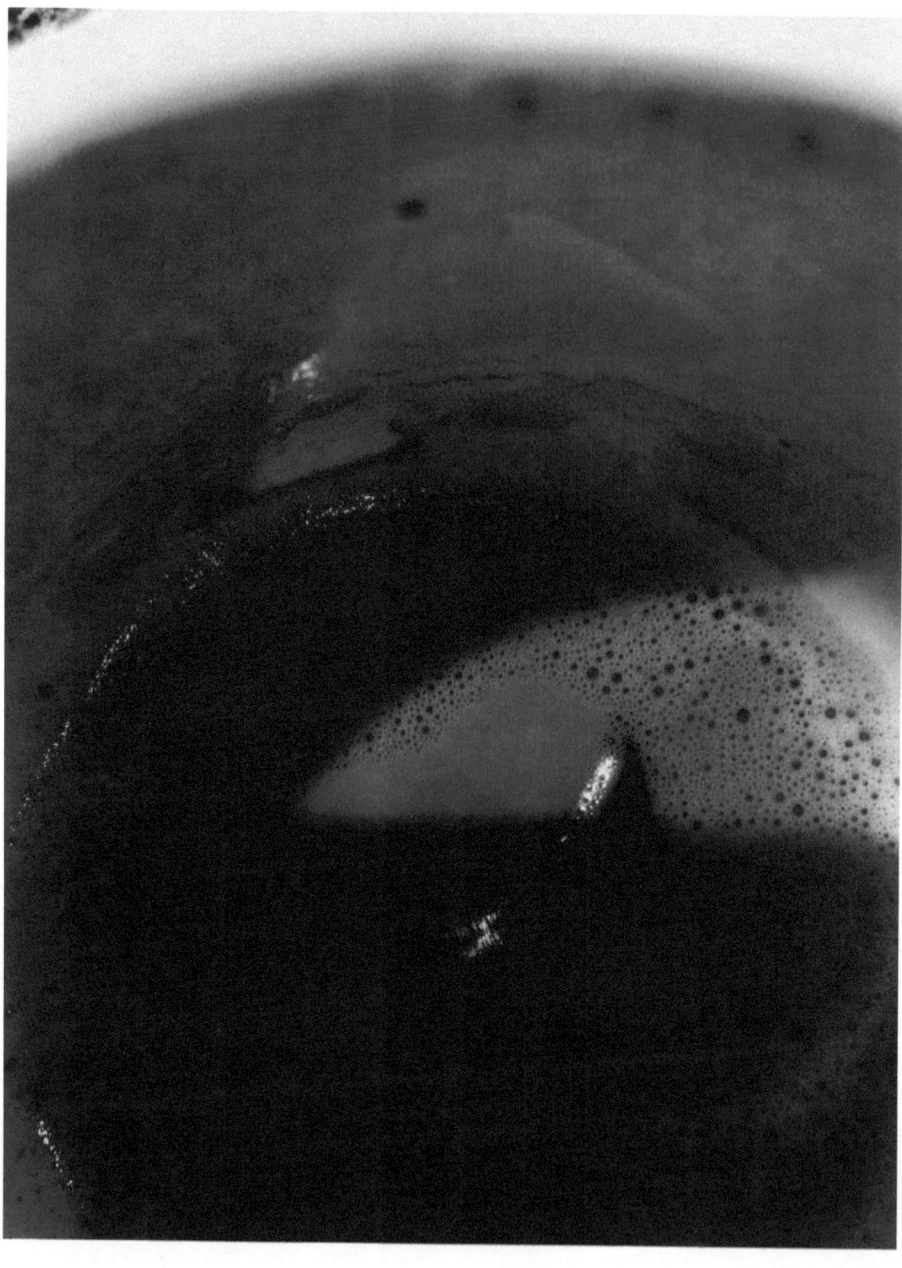

THE FIRST LINE I TOOK FROM NINA SIMONE

what I could do if I had no fear!
how would I do it?
extract the amygdala there are two and they
are almonds but especially on the right
side rip it out with
the fear of anaphylaxis from the one allergic to tree
nuts

fear
ancestors who were fearful
lived because they skirted situations and
said that does not seem safe! while
hiding in caves
but we are safe we are safe in piles of
laundry! still with this fear
having nothing to put it into nothing
to promise a ripping out of
it comes to malaise:

                  I   become
            the   cave.

think about this	strange position!
I am not the one	finding shelter; I am not
the predator; I am the cave!	just swallowing myself
and people may visit, seeking	something;
and I may witness growling	from the outside;
but I do not know	how big I am

CHOOSE YOUR FATE

toward all around the world
it was not that way a coccyx
twist, no:
that was not its turning.

the head knew but wouldn't–
so much that it stamped out its
own house
not fused no but holding

environs change afflict
differently
but a floating hand does the pushing
and your corpus callosum sinks
so sweetly underneath

mired under it all through it and dying
thinking itself hollow but really so deeply and
dead

sinking even when the hand just hovers
deeper with breathing still an
option
a tremble is a world on lips
lips not in it not through it but holding

carrying
like a freight truck:
the dip there lacks depth under a nose
but the mouth oh
the mouth grows gangrene
when it aches to talk
thinking itself holding the world –

have heard it easy to sink
in yourself
but what if world is oblate in a
thyroid

iodine,
metabolize.
tailbone not for twisting

I wish not to choke on a spheroid
but to be an organ donor

RELUCTANT SCIENTIST

So hollow that the wind has to force you to cry
frost tantalizing the ocean behind your eyes when
somewhere deep down, you really wanted to but
now it has all been reduced to
evolution, see

eyes get dry in the cold so
they like to trick you into
sorrow.
Still, you know you wanted to cry.
It took me a while to realize that people can hear me
through this thing we call speaking
but how can it just be this
this thing where
neurons fire in the association cortexes of Wernicke and
Broca's areas which are
both in the left hemisphere of my brain and process
complex languagelogicanddreary
Monday morning algorithms but not
rhythm.
not music.
That's reserved for the right.

But at night I like to imagine it
inhaling my bloodstream,
strumming my spine,

beating in the back of my eyes my
tongue can't quite say why.
But it's just physical,
a fusion of frequencies and waves
how is it the case, that
existential meaning is just the
pinna funneling sound to the
eardrum which vibrates and
translates
through the hammer, anvil and stirrup
roller-coastering through the
semicircular canals and
to the cochlea,
flooding the basilar membrane with fluid and
stimulating tiny little hair cells within it that send
information to nerves that function deeper and
deeper until
what you hear is what you think
but actually only
a mixture of sound patterns that
excited hair cells.

why.
You cry because, suddenly,
folk music won't fill you.
It won't breathe you.
And you keep hoping Bob Dylan will
like he used to.
But this week I'm becoming a reluctant scientist so
don't turn up the stereo.

Sarah Simon

I thought I was so complex.
And, in many ways, I still am,
please,
I know med school isn't a joke.
but I liked to think that laughs were
reverberations of the soul.
So there's pain in knowledge,
in knowing the world more than I want to.
But I still want to;
I like pointing out that weed affects
dopamine that
your heart beats in four
chambers that
nothing's lamer than gossiping but
doing so releases
oxytocin which
forms bonds deep that
you should really get some sleep cuz you're
REM-deprived and you need six or five episodes a night to
streamline what
I'm telling you, to
process this
biology
psychology to
realize that we're all breathtakingly simple.
in the most complex of ways.

Others would tell you to "sleep on it"

HALLOWEEN POEM

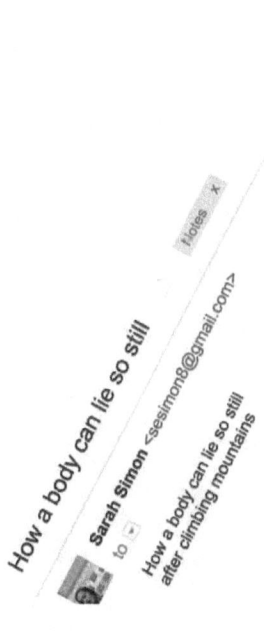

FAMINE IN THE FAMILY

My aunts tell stories and I tell everyone they are crazy.
But I don't want to hear it anymore:
There are five of them, sometimes four
sitting
zigzag along a dinner table,
five Irish bodies,
post-menopause bodies forming a double *v*
there's just a single *u*
and you are surrounded, swallowed
in the mouth of the first *v*,
the zigzag three nearest the porch door.
It is dinnertime in December.

That's solid weight you would be putting on girl.
You space out and think of the space
between your thighs,
the girl is
in
a
space they probably can't hear: *Where is your mind at?*
The girl listening to the gap, not
eating right!
They are waiting for her
to come back
to the conversation,
to show up

to the dinner table,
to show up
to the hearty stuff
at the dinner table.
The aunts are waiting for their girl to
come back,
show up,
and sit down her solid weight.
Finish your plate. What are we having tomorrow?

They are again already planning. Already planning can you
pass the salad?
Finish your plate.
What are we having tomorrow?

They hand me the bowl I know
is just a short-term filler, really:
Salad can make your plate look full, abounding, a bounty.
But it doesn't fill. Your body is a famine –
but your aunts, they are green goddesses.
They make the pour of dressing seem slow and
easy.
That wasn't so hard, *was it?*

But I said no to the dressing.
I told them I never liked dressing anyway.
But really it was all the oil it had all
that fat!
I press my tailbone into the wood of my dinnertime seat:
They are already planning.

That's solid weight girl. Eat your steak –
I am running to the store tonight, what are we having for dinner tomorrow?
But I didn't want steak today.
Yet, it is not a problem because of this.
It is a problem
I am a problem
because of Irish heritages.
At dinnertime with my aunts,
it is the ultimate form of disrespect:

She won't eat, she's not eating
enough, look at her!
Not look at you.
Look at her! *Look at* our girl!
I thought of when they were girls.

Of course the photos of the five back in '65 all
lined
up
in black-and-white
solid weight
in black-and-white, *hard*
and learning.
Learning of their parents' famines.
Developing a fear of famines.
Developing a hard fear of famines of
being incomplete of not
having enough to eat of not
being solid enough to sustain –

learning. Learning of
hard times
in the '30s. Of
eating off every dime waiting
for the milkman eating
out of cans dressing
up the Spam! these
are
hard
lessons
for soft babies.

From the photo, you can tell how many
potatoes they'd eaten before.
You can tell how many times they'd seen
the eyes of their mother quiver
at not having enough to provide not
eating right
quite enough getting
instead dependent
on potato juice.
If only it had not been so cold.
If only we had sewed our sock-holes –
If we had only enough money to eat:
A family history of famine.

But now we are comfortable Irish people
in the Midwest.
Famine is not the problem.
In all this excess I am choosing what to eat,

to stay skinny.
This makes me the *princess*: I have the nerve to stay skinny!
This makes me the *problem*.
But I have a problem! I want to be skinny!
So skinny so to be gone.
She won't eat, she's not eating
enough, look at her!
Not look at you.
Look at our girl!
Look at her!
So I looked at her too:

I saw her at the dinner table.
I saw her pass the bread on.
I saw her refuse the steak away,
I saw her salad-camouflage her plate.

You know we are already planning a meal for tomorrow,
like our fathers did,
like our Irish fathers did –
what stories are you listening to?
We told you how mom used to stack up on cans and cram
us
fill *us*
with
potatoes.
Don't you know that we have to eat?

It is the greatest hypocrisy of the family,
which tries its best to fill you.

But if they had just heard the famine filling my soul,
the voices stealing fat and bounty
from my bones.
All cold. Hard and cold.

Yes, I am sick.
Yes,
like the way your grandfather died of potato juice
and your mother became a psychiatrist.
Can you be my psychiatrists?
I promise the reason I don't eat is not to spite the family tree

EXCUSES BECOME MUSES

and make you moo like a moose
but moose don't moo!
bemused by
yourself.
do.

Isn't it remarkable that your daughter
has grown into this speculative being?
sometimes I wonder if you muse on that

all the same I want you to forget it
enough to meet me for eggs benedict
and let me complain when the yolks don't run

DRINK YOUR MILK

they see us going through cycles
the wise, the older;
but circular is the type of thinking we circumvent;
for we are always progressing.

it's nice to think that milk
couldn't help
even though they told us so;
we are growing, yes, but we are grown;
read
my
bone
plates–
I breathed them into smoke

and we calcify each other anyway
with experience
    touching too early
    dying too early
but feeling all the while
in the tonic water
some sort of advantage.

you see,
we don't bother ourselves with the *expected*

age-appropriate
milieus. we don't drink milk
we always feel different
and our eye bags become edema
for dreams.

(now I am diagnosing)
we are artists and we are diagnosing.

really
is everyone just pretending or are they really

finding serenity in those things

a head garnishes my exterior
we are artists.

you prop my shoulders up
just enough to maintain
a tasteful slouch.
we are artists.

I don't enunciate, my life is too heavy.
excuse me. I am an artist.

we are artists we are so

what. SO
WHAT? I forgot how to do
long division, love.

Sarah Simon

sure, I write poems
and peer inside but this house of
homes,
these bones are empty.

really
what do I do
really? as an artist.
do I get anything done?
are they there
do they exist do you
feel these bones
on you
these bones these homes these
poems
are they anywhere but
in me
do you hear them
let's talk

EQUATIONS, NO ART.

I remember Whitman when fearing statistics

he dreaded astronomy lectures but looked up after

so sound to
not listening sipping
synchronicity
no causes

formulas saying so from
below

M. Waldman, who inspirited
Frankenstein
facts, experiments, with atoms.

is this art now
this stringency we breathe in regiments
is this art now
to terrorize with certainty?
is this art

now
palms extensions of a brain
they reach it they rest it

on a mandible.
how could I even think without my bones

mathematicians coming in and saving everyone
"here is the equation,"

glasses intersecting the V of his eye
from the side
palms on a dining room table plane his
brain and everything I don't know.

after he is finished expounding
I sip my tea
I did not pour the honey into it;
he plucks a pretzel from the table dish.

what if there lies an algorithm to its knots
I know he doesn't want to say
I say I don't want to know
until I do

HOUSE OF LIMBS NOT LITURGIES

this thing is bland
it was Christmas Eve and she was taking a Spanish lesson
on Duolingo.
to be efficient and active she tapped tenses while squatting,
pulsing, gy-
rating from the belly.
she learned Spanish while belly dancing.
mom walked in,
what are you doing?
my Spanish lesson.
oh
I like to do squats while doing it
this one is about religion,
like espíritu and
religiosa
uh-huh
what you're doing doesn't match.
oh momma
if anything
the body is the religion.

my mother would take us to church
late
she got caught up in solitaire.
this isn't to comment on religious
canons or queens

or my mother,
who sails by a safe
tardy
indefinitely. this
is of

late.
to being late when the digital
the gps
the seven alarms go off and we
get caught up.

not the kind that's
warranted –
inconvenienced.
but the belated that's satiated
doing what it does

in the moment I
thought of her solitaire how selfish
it seemed
to scrap the homily for digital stringency
cards
the taut faces unwound her
back she
sat
up
straight
if to slap an ace
of spades she was
a decompressing queen
of diamonds

but what was she doing being late like that I
thought mass was necessary she said she did too but really how
could she deprave by a computer game I
was nine I prayed every night because I thought GOD would
harm me
everyone would die if I didn't I didn't understand was she
killing MY chance for sanctity with her solitaire?!!???

don't get caught up, she
spoke from a computer
chair.
you are your own house for holy.

it was Midnight mass that same Christmas evening
people singing
joy to the world
and the eucharistic acclamation
held up the body, the
bread.
and the line was leading she
led herself
to that body,
palms open for comfort and feeling
amen
and she turned to the right,
passed the wine-goblin eyes
she could have sworn he noticed how
she kept it
this thing
oughta be inspected.

HOW BEAUTIFUL IT IS TO BE HUNGRY –

not to be dying of
it, but rather
to be wanting that
scrumptious crumb of
survival.
and how sad it is
to not be it,
for having eaten
to surfeit.

being hungry in
Spanish isn't
the same as being
it in English.
because in English,
you don't have it, but
rather you are it
in English, it's not going to
grip and pass you, but rather
it's going to characterize you
and in Spanish, if you're
with hunger, you're with it,
her.

her, your friend
that brings you
sweets
and gossip
of the past week-
end.

how desperate it is
to be hungry in English
because in its language,
that friend is never
going to part
to plant and grow, swallow
herself
whole
with what she finds
in her own field.
no,
regrettably English
refers
not to the thing
that gives life,
but to the mouth that eats it

QUE BELLO ES TENER HAMBRE,

no estar muriendo
de ella sino
estar queriendo esa migaja
sabrosa de sobrevivencia.
y que tan triste es no tenerla
por haber comido
demasiado.

tener hambre en español no
es el mismo de
tenerla en inglés.
porque en inglés no la
tienes, sino la estás
en inglés no te va a pasar,
sino te va a caracterizar.
y en español, si estás con
hambre, estás con ella,
ella.
ella tu amiguita
que te trae

golosinas
y el chisme
del fin de semana pasada.

que desesperado es
tener al hambre en inglés
porque en su lengua,
esa amiguita nunca
te va a despedir
para sembrar y crecer,
ensimismar-
se
de lo que encuentre
en su campo propio.
no,
lamentablemente
en el inglés
se refiere
no a la cosa que da vida,
sino a la boca que la coma

ΔΔ

DECISIONS DIAMOND TO OBSERVERS

but they don't know the turmoil behind the
good and
evil,
duality hurts.
it
cuts close. runs
through. aches like doubt
in a rocking chair.
such a thing to ever be sure of anything
but to appear so to act and say to move effusively
a hip bend its own symphony pledging crystal maybe
don't think about it. so much doubt don't
think about it. even doing good (what is thought to be)
hear about it.
rocking hurts it's nauseating I
don't want to question my
hips or anyone's they're only
clear without contemplated obscurity
tempered. fair-minded. virtues themselves
yes no truths yes but why do we listen to music
why do we swear by externals validity bestowed by proxies
hips please a proxy for your   heart
to move without question
stirring consequences–
lack of balanced

reasoning. but the act of it won't hurt
as much.
and a slap after satisfies
I'm slapping myself from the inside
believing in nothing weighing thought over action maybe both
are good.
but I will believe tonight don't shield your bones
baby nothing is valid without transcending
shame please,
no shame. no second-
guessing
prick your lips on the apex of diamond hips your
bones are so clear they're aching you're rocking
slapping sovereignty
no just
pay for it later
or see that you never had to in the first place.
we impound ourselves by false judges
thought is not true
but we are authentic. your
hips are not archives.
they are pounding lectures flipping over
rocking chairs they stand, broad.
open like holy communion hands we take bread.
but who is handing it? don't question don't
question it's just a cracker cross yourself it's
all in god no questions god bend and
pray.
but the blood wine is crystallized in a belly button

sip from it
choruses in shimmying
being is to think and not at all
do for yourself without validation from
another you are a house your
stubble is true don't
pick at worry that it looks
sloppy oh my god who
is handing you the fucking cracker

OUR BODIES ARE THE UNSPOKEN AGREEMENTS

our brains evolved to complement our
bodily survival we are not logical
but we can be
we are not tame
but we can be

"it is the international summit of the
human genome project to-day!"
there was a tickle in her throat that raised
to a snicker from her nose.

want a snicker bar?
huh
smile
hah.

the world is ending

WHAT TO DO WITH TENDENCIES HOLD

"Nothing from nothing leads nothing
You gotta have SOMETHING
If you wanna be with me."

Billy Preston never strayed too far from his gospel roots
And the thing is he fooled me that I had
them or he helped me grin
to them like
I knew
them

HE CARRIES HIS TENDENCIES
Remembered for a gap-toothed grin yes and loose limbs
yes what to do with tendencies

Yes
what to do with tendencies hold
me
Half-assed made beds do not offer the duvet cover at
night.
They do not offer the duvet.

Did Billy ever perform half-heartedly and feel cold at night
did he ever make his bed did the choirs
teach him to?

Sarah Simon

Make your bed and lie in it.

What to do with tendencies
"Will it go around in circles
Will it fly high like a bird up in the sky?"

Soft fine fluffy feathers taken from
ducks.
Shut up, you don't think of that when you hold it.
Shut up, you don't think of that
you've never touched a duck or even ordered it from Peking
I always thought that meant the thing would be squinting
when it came out,
steaming

What to do with tendencies
that carry over to your
heart
Billy died when his pericardium–

pericardium | ˌperiˈkärdēəm |
noun (pl. **pericardia** | -ˈkärdēə |) Anatomy
the membrane enclosing the heart, consisting of an outer fibrous layer and an inner double layer of serous membrane.

THAT WHICH ENCLOSED HIS HEART INFLAMED
Pericarditis
Late in 2005
He fell into a coma.
Never regained consciousness.

What to do with tendencies, hold
me.
They will kill me too.
If I do what I am
what I enflame
up on stage
it will kill me too.
So when I'm dying just think about it;
maybe my brain blew up

ASPIRE

human   anatomists
are
romantic
they put
the moon
in the
heart and
it is crescent:
semilunar,
they
call
it

WIND NECESSITATES TEMPESTUOUS

you are like standing in a room with the wind.

you are like french-braiding my hair in the wind,
on an enclosed roof.

i try not to sin with the strands
build them thicker, collect a triad make them easier
to hold.

but you are wisping,
knotting,
complicating my fingers.
i am pulling you and you speak french but do not braid
let me upbraid
you
and knot you with,
knot you in the wind.

it was never you, not you, it was the knot in the wind

it is on you i keep tugging
but you are a wisp! you are too thin
i cannot upbraid the wind because i
stand with it too, I cannot
walk out of this room

VV (FANGS; I'M HUNGRY)

what has who, the
coffee-stained limping
virgin
of virtues.
she limps to quip speed.
there's no need to drink
coffee for
caffeine – it just

feels good and looks right on a
continental night,
the naïveté pounding
from your temples
supersedes the
northern lights.
you're

alright.
I
like you.
you squeeze me a virgin of
my virtues.
they don't have me anymore.

RAW

I know what it means to feel raw. Like the
crunch of a fresh apple or the sizzling
of pink chicken in a pan.
CrunchmybonesSizzlemysoulMakemefeel raw, like
the first moment you admired my eyelids

COLLARBONE

Jagged on the edges,
you come forth.
Jumping off of ledges,
we morph.

Nothing but blankness,
as clear as your skin.
An element of safeness,
not there, but within.

Cheeks are rosy now,
so tall, so thin.
I wonder not why, but how
transfixed by a sin.

Momentum never fails,
nor does the crash.
So, off we sail
with your collarbone lash.

YOU CAN'T EAT DESSERTS FOREVER

mmmm, honey sugar,
you with your leaping lids of
rain,
you nut case,
dressed in white chocolate

macadamia raging the brain causing
cavities
in your
paranoid sweet

tooth pondering the preheat the
rise
the butter the
battered drain and

the time.

My lustful lids' rhyme.
what do they see?

heat, my sweet.
enough to singe the oneirism
of matrimonial butter-
cream.

perhaps the toothpick inserts too
easily
and the gesticulating tongues begin
to sear with

youthful,
auspicious,
Carpe Diem fear.

this is all
too
hasty, so
let our burning cool on a rack
of steel and
give it
time:

that which be the shriveling salt of
all things supple
but can create some new
flavor
and call it
a
pickle.

VACUUM DIET (ON BINGE EATING)

crinkle-cut fries lonesome pies
I am gorging
on hills.

jaws
graze   valleys
I   am
ascending   as vacuum
consuming   sloping

imagining   my limbs
as corners   of a carpet
spread li-   ke Arabia

ashamed until   shameless
to expose   armpits
and stre-   tch out,
belly   loose

I want   forever
to be   a vacuum
never to   spit anything
out but   just to
consume.

FOR TWO MONTHS, EVERY MEAL FOSTERED A FEAR OF BABIES

month 1: Type II if.
I am carrying a pregnancy test
and held at a stop sign.
this one holds you for particularly long.
it is about to change
it's green

Δ

month 2: cada puerta, cada ventana.
think positive
of the winter you promised yourself you'd
learn to play the harmonica
of the winter you will lie
down, cradling myself to comfort
but more to elicit sympathy from the
lady when she comes back.
sinking in the throes of helplessness I
had not shared with mother,
which was odd.
usually I talked and she sweetened me up with bee debris
she would hold me and say
"honey."
but when you are your own fetus, with

SEX SYMBOLS

The vagina's natural chemical balance is at a pH of about 4.5 – the same acidity of red wine. The uterus is a pear-shaped organ.

Ovaries are about the size and shape of almonds! Want to prevent cysts? Eat their shapes. But let's not deviate too far from the penis: The corona and frenulum are crown and underside the glans is an acorn head, fall for it! Only a trick to keep it all going. Your prostate is the size and shape of a walnut! 200-500 million sperm travel with orgasmic and fructose the from vesicle but seminal comprise only 1% of what comes out! In the fourth century, Aristotle said erection is chiefly caused by

scuraum, eringoes, cresses, crymon, parsnips, artichokes, turnips, asparagus, candied ginger, acorns bruised in powder and drunk muscadel, scallion, sea shell fish, etc

maybe possibly one in you it
holds you. so I imagined the lady was my surrogate
and that her words would ooze, soothe.
she would now be a mother.
and Nora had satellite disks in her eyes
quiet sighs
slowly pressing her thigh into the mint green cushion
when she walked in,
handing me a cup to pee in.
we silently agreed a negative was
preferred, but she left saying,
"think positive."
and maybe paused behind the door,
wishing to retract, then telling herself,
"she knows what
I thought of the Spanish classes I had taken for seven years.
I liked infinitives, they could split.
And I never thought of English that way, with
form tenses and hyphenated changes
listed in the
yo
tú
ella/él/usted
nosotros
vosotros
ellas/ellos
I dissected any word by that order,
it was quite lovely yes to look through
the subjects and the people
for an answer.

and of course the thought of easy view
lent to sonogram dreams:
could I even count on this pee?
procedures and their accuracies
I need to read through be looked through
I need to be wiped clean
is this heaviness of me a baby or bagel cream?
Nora, I am looking at you to look through me.
she jiggled in she was the ultimatum of
a door knob it was similar to
orgasm it was the pent up angry little ball lactating from the possibility
the negative was the positive
that the red light was a type II and the
traffic lanes had changed.
a stutter, something growing inside
and choking on the things I metabolize
sucking it in may kill the peaceful little thing!
peacefully I wanted it to die.
Nora, no.
NO
no.
it's your body.

Δ

and I pushed out of that door, out of that room as if
to push out of every fucking

Δ

cada puerta, cada ventana:
every door, and every window
is an endogenous little watershed
of the belly.
situations are exited through the abdomen.
don't suck it in –
every gaze down is wondering if it's
really food.

and this all will spill from the fallow bodies
paralleled by feeling:
slowly opening and closing each other like doors and
windows,
on a beach.
when you think you can see everything

ΔΔΔ

GOING UNDER

∂

The dinner is tired
like wiping the marks of a bowl from the table but not
from the bottom of the bowl and
setting the bowl down again.

                                         sit and issues are brought up,
                         stay and they are carried over.

Dialogue is placed by elbows and
fingertip-topped to pyramids
people talk and seem to be praying:
you praise their nails and respond with your hierarchy

and you believe in your argument,
(which adds a different perspective).
You wait to be called the Messiah, or
the dinnertime pharaoh.

But auntie yawns
and maybe the pork could have been cooked better!
Did you hear, they call it the other white meat?

Sarah Simon

μ

The mall is lethargy
like setting a handbag down on a table-
clothed table that is red
that is now infested with the bottom of your bag.

       exhale and the items are heavy,
      inhale and innocence ends.

You spend a wallet baby on Dead Sea mineral bath products
to please a painstaker:
she stands out here so long just waiting

and you believe you are different,
(trying to think of her as the same).
You wait with her to the end of the pitch, or
until her eyes die.

Together you yawn
and maybe she is saving up for school
so you expend masochistically
Did you know deceased riverbeds keep you young?

®

The room is weary
like closing a drawer to feel like you did
something then remembering its contents
were the reason you walked in the room,

CORE COLLECTION

⌐

leaning forwards in a restaurant to let
a waiter pass but you don't
scoot your chair in and
under,

॰

seeing all forms of life writhing in front of yours already,
I think Kafka talked about that.
Yes, he had a good quote.

†

Your thigh,
when brought to its utmost verticality:
right-angled to your hips
with the tibia fibula propping
straightens all the *S*s of the ancient present:
the hunk of skin-flesh just under the knee rounds out;
the mid-femur curves in
just to curve out again. But it is recent of you to call it flabby.
Well yes, I say, you have skin.

∂

Always trying to get around the core of it:

"ok it's dinner let's pray

Sarah Simon

father
son
holy spirit amen
lalalalala *ok*."

She reddens and grins–
swipes a cross from forehead to chest
        across the neck!
        of this history:

The glowing hand of my mother
who went to Catholic school.
now rushes the tradition because she's
hungry!
"I'm sorry world," she says,
"I am hungry and *tired*."

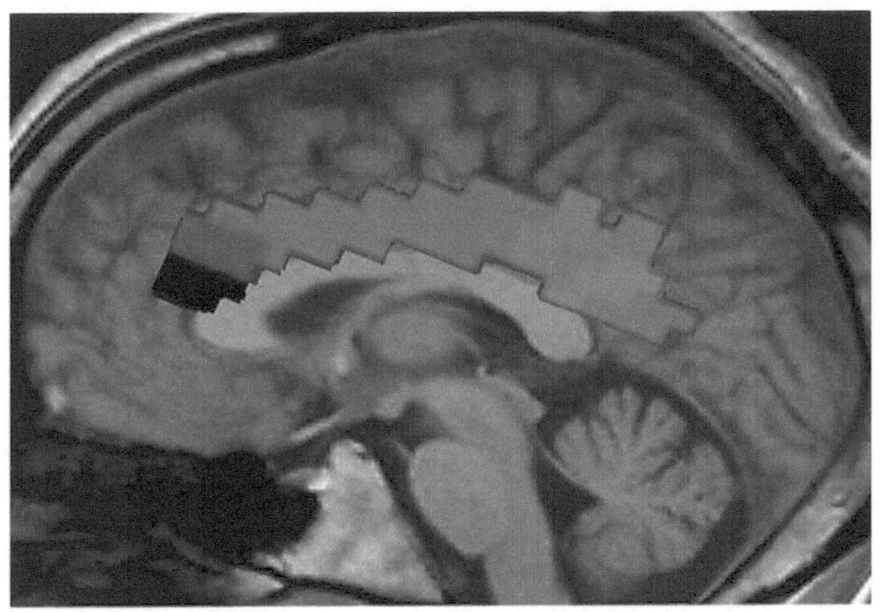

It is an integral part of the limbic system, which is involved with emotion formation and processing,[1] learning,[2] and memory.[3][4] The combination of these three functions makes the cingulate gyrus highly influential in linking behavioral outcomes to motivation (e.g. a certain action induced a positive emotional response, which results in learning).[5] This role makes the cingulate cortex highly important in disorders such as depression[6] and schizophrenia.[7]

CINGULUM

wraps to form a cranial
bay curve
table
winding from that
Boston Bostonian

    I am not a New Englander but Cape Cod's shiver

hooks.
above is that Merrimack of mine
and skiing and reading,
collapsing into the cortex of itself, laughing:

>*He is saying his haircut is always $16*
>*and when paying*
>*he only asks for a dollar back*

                        There is not depression;

>*You "thank you" through a drawl drawn*
>*out and down with the staircase,*
>*to a door held open for you that*
>*you expect to be held open for you*

                        There is hope in you expecting;

CORE COLLECTION

Art!

There is a silence after screams.

You are etched on my heart

DEFINITION

1 engrave (metal, glass, or stone) by coating it with a
protective layer, drawing on it with a needle, and then
covering it with acid to attack the parts the needle
has exposed, especially in order to produce prints
from it: (as adj. **etched**)*: etched glass windows.*

There is the feeling come back.

There is far too much feeling.

So I will go away from it now
and vacation on the cape playing hand
games with anchors;
serotonin is the masthead and my boat is upside-down

So the anchors will dock in my direction,
and I will have a will to entertain them,
with whispers. of little things the people around me do,
curving to drown a family secret:

planning and expecting and art and feeling,
laying beach chairs out over the hook
and an umbrella,
to protect from the sun.

Their little ticks are the curlicues
drawing on banalities concentrically, while
depressed people only draw on themselves.

Depressed people twist for nothing.
        Depressed people know they know everything.
            Depressed people are more realistic.

            Depressed people neither maintain tip rituals nor
        Drawl to held-open doors nor create;
Depressed people are not in love.

            (Am I depressed)
                ?

Definitions are what is known
in parses.
Wrap the cingulum by a numb-numbing curve, and
accept the prehensile word. eat clam
chowder.

Would 6 be a good time for dinner?
            Feels like I'll be hungry by then

(You are quite good at monitoring the
activity of your duodenum)
(It's nice to know you care about things)

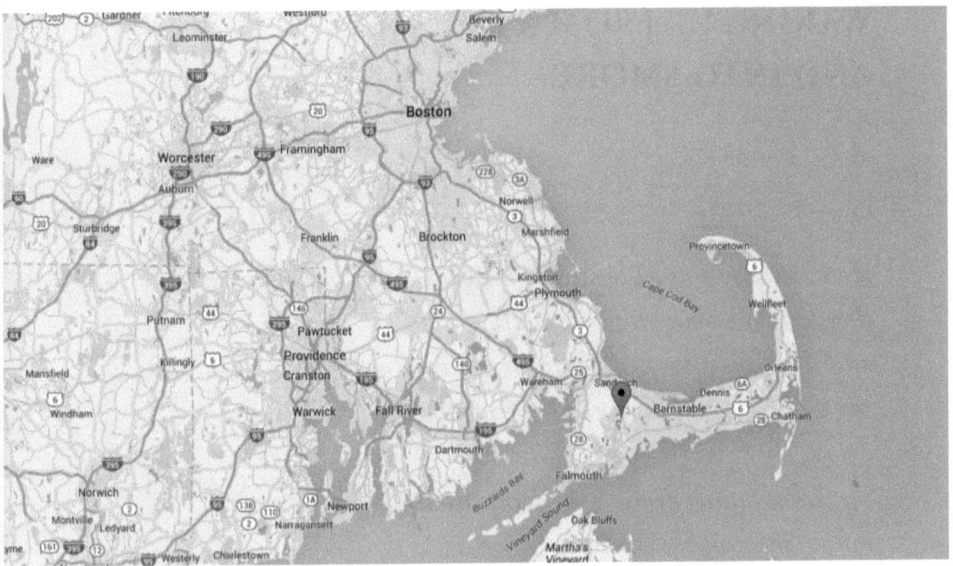

Credit to google maps

WAKING UP FROM A DREAM AND INTO SMOKE

*there was one point I looked at the clouds they weren't moving
they were removing it was peaceful
and then this stream of panic pressed into
me that they were supposed to be moving —*

*my day spinning around me going around
me my focusing too much
too much on us too much for moving fine and they knocked me
out I almost scratched my arm to stop myself to get out
of the habit;*

        prying open a container lid,
        I put something in my coffee:
        I wake up not knowing myself;
        cinnamon reminds me.

    why do smokers' voices sometimes deepen ?
        there is an edge to you,
        an edge to you and
        through it seethes
        insecurities;

CORE COLLECTION

there is a corpulence cultivated in bone marrow
and from the stairway, you look quite fat
and I like that, your teeth –
you are so yellow!

be young with me as I make you vegan pancakes

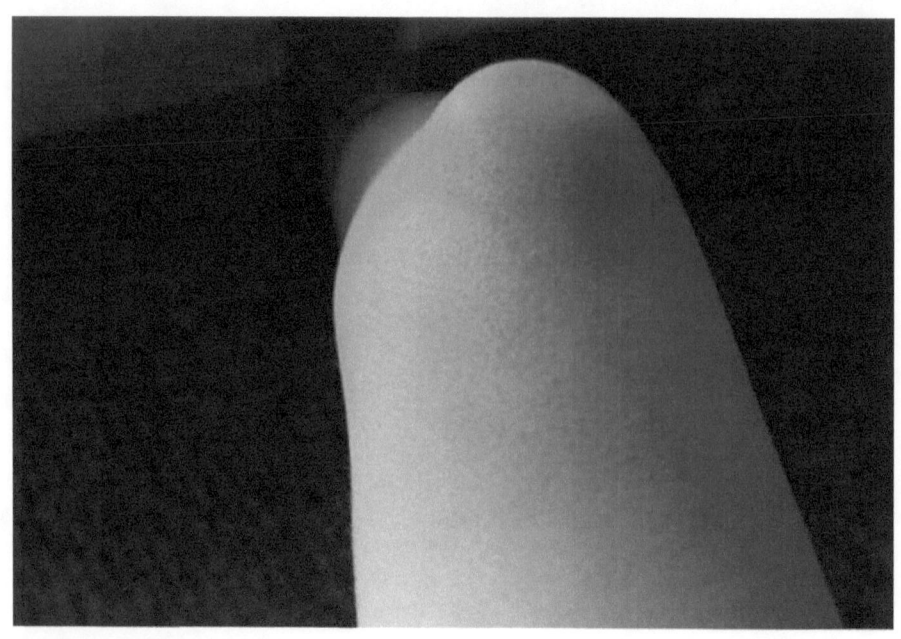

THE PECULIAR PAIN OF EXAMINING A MAP

an atlas evokes a certain nothingness
or rather rips a certain
something from your
sternum.
eyelashes
burn them, the
innermost nothings,
roving around as the
wind.

high pressure never descended
the mind never mended a
treaty with the world.

HOW TO READ A MAP

what to do with a map
when it is agony?
proffering so much but
the eyes won't take it
they want to yearn to but
cower, staring
visual recluse,
can't reproduce.

atlas
expanse as expander
of awareness
did you see there
were mountains?

staring staring but at surfeit;
the mind is a caldera
imploding the mouth drops
kissing the earth –
that happens in
Wyoming.

at face want all of it
know it seize it,
hang it on a wall

seeming of I; no it is
not of I that's why the
memory falters:

to remind that
understanding is not
laid out for you!
eyes cannot scroll
contextualize
the whole at a single
sternum-crushing glance;

they must rove, sip like
winds
name them touch
with own atlas of
recognition.

it is not laid out for you,
I;
so we must spit terrain
and chew it,
pack our own sediment,
watch it settle.

CORE

it really is the fear that you will not be able to stop, that
which snarls you into thinking of salads and
eating and planning around calories,
exercise, not
plans,
not people
not events
not even yourself —

it really is the fear that you will not be able to stop, that
that voice, *it is not even*
a voice, that
CACOPHONY whistling through the soul and hollowing it,
disemboweling and
filling the esophagus
the stomach
the large intestine with wind,

nothing but wind! a cold and newly-bought vacuum bag
body,
brittle and sinking bones to have condoned by side gazes
and magazine pages,
and the messages that you have now swallowed inside-out,
vomited into the rigidity of your day and into the rigidity
of yourself —
yourself —
it really is the fear that you will not be able

to stop yourself from eating and swelling
like a Missouri mother in Wal-Mart;

it really is the fear that you will not be able to
accept your tummy for the Missouri mother it
wants to be, the amount it wants to eat;

it really is the fear that you will not like yourself,
know yourself enough
to calm down,
chill out,
say, "I've had enough, thank you, only one piece or
serving or
helping or
glass of wine…"

it really is the fear that you cannot be "normal," that is
pace yourself, like
your mother, who always leaves a few crumbs on her plate;

it really is the realization that there are only two
ways for you to feel fulfilled, fill yourself:

- eat everything,
- eat nothing;

it is the fear that you will not be able to handle
anything in-between, the balance that life requires itself,
yourself —

so you die, you die you die after everyone
has already attended your open casket,
met your skeleton

DARÉ A LUZ A UNA SOLEDAD

a una hija mía que se llama
así porque hoy día, aprendí
otra vez
las dos razones de dar
a una chiquilina en sus
primeros respiros de vida
esta supuesta maldición:

ella, ella no vale la pena,
la soledad, amiga mía;
que debajo su sol, se quema;
que dentro de su
casa, no hay nadie
más

I WILL GIVE TO LIGHT, BIRTH, TO A SOLEDAD

to a daughter of mine
whose name is so because
today, i learned again
the two reasons to
give a little girl in her
first breaths of life
this supposed curse:

she's just not worth
it, loneliness,
my friend; her sun burns;
there's no one inside
of her house

y cómo puede ser que me
sienta sola yo enfrente
de una mesa llena con
gente rodeada por gente,
sintiéndome sola, como si
estuviera la única allí para
disfrutar de la comida?

aprendí
de nuevo, se me
ocurrió
que su raíz aparece y crece
en la casa del espantoso
malvado miedo de tenerla.
así, temiéndola empiezas
a ser rebelde;
empiezas a rechazar lo
que la gente te llame;

empiezas a ponerse
más flaca, más linda,
más lo que sea;
para que la gente te ame.

and how can it be that
i feel so lonely in front
of a table full of people,
surrounded by
people,
feeling alone, as if i
were the only one there
to enjoy the food?

i learned
again, it occurred to me
that its root appears
and grows
in the house of the
haunting, evil fear
of being it.
like that, fearing it,
you start to become
rebellious. you start to
reject whatever people
seem to want to
call you.

you start to get
skinny, pretty,
more of whatever –
so that people
love you.

pero en este lío
desesperado, lo que
hagas la perpetua.
lo que haces
por rechazar la comida le da
de comer.

quizás esta es la
contradicción más hermosa:
que no te das de comer,
para evitarla, mientras
le das de comer a ella
tu mente misma
tu cuerpo, tu sol,
your soul, brillante. y como
una chica, una chiquilina
en el jardín,

but in
this desperate mess,
precisely what you do to
avoid her perpetuates her.
what you do to reject
food feeds her.

maybe this is the most
beautiful contradiction:
that you do not feed
yourself to avoid
her while giving
her everything – your mind
your body your sun,
your soul, shining.
and like a girl, a little
girl in the garden,

Sarah Simon

siempre la vas a temer
mientras estás rodeada por
risas. siempre vas a temer
a ella, como en el jardín.

y como ya se me fue *my
soul*, le voy a dar a mi
hija el nombre de ella

1.) mayormente por su
apodo del Sol lindo.
para que ella, mi alma,
tenga un lugar
para descansar y crecer;
mientras la hija mía siempre
mantenga su calor.
cursi, ya sé;

you're always going to fear
her while you're surrounded
by laughter. you're always
going to fear her,
like in the garden.

and since my soul
has already gone, i'll
give my daughter
her name

1.) mostly for her
nickname, Sol.
so that she, my
soul, has a place
to rest and grow,
while my daughter always
maintains her heat.
cheesy, i know;

que salió entre susurros
oscurecidos
desde bocas que ni
conocen, que ni ninguna
vez van a conocer
a la profundidad con que
muerden sus muelas
y hacen de ella una
comida, una delicadeza;

but so that when
she becomes rebellious
(because my daughter will
be a rebel, there's no doubt)
she'll fight against
her, loneliness,
a light already seen said
given known, from
her first breaths
and isn't introduced
to her like i was, the
shadow of a threat
leaking light between
whispers, contours, dark
-ness, mouths
that will never meet the
deep of their teeth;
making a food, a delicacy

2.) pero también
para que cuando se
convierta en rebelde
(porque la hija mía va ser
rebelde, es indudable)
luche contra ella,
ella una luz ya
vista, dicha, dada, sabida
desde sus primeros respiros
y que no sea presentada
con ella como fue yo, la
amenaza mía ensombrecida

out of her;

ella quien
de repente se
muera, cuando por fin tenga
un lugar de nombrar y
tener puesto, lado a lado
su miedo más profundo
y los rayos
con que debería
haber brillado

she, who
suddenly dies, when
finally she finds
a place to name and
lie, side by side,
her deepest fear and the rays
with which she always
should have shined

DIS –

Dis the convenience of vision; dis the utility of a left hand;
dis the neuroticisms of a more normal network; dis the
dearth of hyperactivity; dis the existence of your right
kidney –

dis my ability to live without yours –
it happens all the time, but is understood differently: simply,
a disability. It is understood as the word.

But if I had three fingers
on my dominant hand –
would that not be the same as looking down at your set,
wishing they had gotten you into a band?

If I had dyslexia,
taking the adjectives for verbs –
would that not be the same as you
spelling my thinking into "absurd"?

If I had a stutter
and could not speak straight in verse –
would that not be the same as you not speaking with me at
all?
Which would be worse?

Sarah Simon

If I were deaf
and could not hear the city sirens yell –
would that not be the same as you not learning,
for the emergency of my inclusion,
basic ASL?

If I could not eat without counting calories
and starved myself thin –
would that not be the same as you dismissing
the obsession exposing my ribs?

And if I had autism,
with an inability to experience empathy –
would that not be the same as you looking at me
as a disability?

Now look back down at your hands.

Imagine doing something you had always wanted to with them.

Imagine playing in a band.

But you
never had the practice!
You never had the time –
you never had the mother who pressed your hand onto her keyboard,
or the teacher who accorded you rhythm and rhyme.

CORE COLLECTION

In dyslexia,
I never had standard hemispheric activation;
my stutter could have developed for many reasons;
deaf from birth,
I never had my cochlea fluid push the stereocilia into sound;
in anorexia, I never developed a healthy perception of pounds;
and my autism –
I never could isolate one cause.
It has influenced who I am,
separated me from who I never was.

So dis my ability
to make do with and
cope with and
recover from
what has never been done:
Pick up a cheap ukulele at the record store,
and strum.

MÁS QUE YO

Aida is trimming the tree in Quito and I decide to assist—
yet, the stretching of limbs comes to rip and
reminds me of how thin
I am. because suddenly I cannot—

retreat the bed to rest and soon come to
fever, later she looks at me the way you look at a blood moon
the moon, a moon,

my moon—
at dinner she keeps on questioning *esta fiebre*
and I look into her eyes to see you,
the silence of that rock is the only thing
I know you have to look at,
the only thing that mocks the silence I feel from—

two days later, I recount the illness to a Luis
and he grins, oh yes, *el cuerpo es muy inteligente, no?*
I laugh until I think of some way to—

> *your body was always this way, internalizing to*
> *appear sane before the breaking out into*
> *does mine do that, too?* A
> veces me duele la izquierda pierna, y no
> estoy segura exactamente por qué—

and you cried in my lap when you felt
the bend in your back snapping
schism of that week you left I felt mine too,
and four months later, I'm still not sure exactamente por qué.

If I can't figure, then does the body—
why exactly did it feel a need to boil?
I laugh, I shrug, I admit
to the majesty of its messages,
what it may want to tell me this Christmas:
oh yes,

it will boil my brain without me knowing why,
rattle *la cabeza*,
pitbull inside a *jaula*—
cleaning out the *porquería*,
the things no longer serving me.

its killing will
its killing you will in
the end keep me alive—
sí, ya lo sé Luis,
es más inteligente que yo.

WOOSH!

      the gray of humanity whitewashes
          the wrong; the orange,
            the red, parts of
             the wind's
              song:

               a
             bitten
           comment,
         teeth in grief;
      their quibbles, their quarrels:
but just stale gusts in   the blowing of things

ALWAYS MENTION THE NUTS

panhandling for food

she wore camouflage

emptying weakness

on the train just

out of
army,
no
job.

it was Black Friday

bloated potatoes
above
her, surrounding
her

she suggested leftovers. out of
money,
no
job.

she begged for warmth not currency.

I recalled:
bread
over my
shoulder,

cranberry walnut toasting
tin foil,
left
over.

can you
eat nuts?

oh no!

*but
thank
you.*

why are you so beautiful? she
moaned.
I begged for her
belly

BOILING WATER

when I discovered boiling water
I drank it to suppress hunger to help me
not eat.

and when extant tonsils grew sore,
I drank boiling water to direct the burn;
with lemons, it helps you learn.

when I discovered lemons
I squeezed them to jump-start my
metabolism

in the morning,
I squeezed lemons to offset the distending
of my hips, who broaden by their sending

messages, to me:

she never drank with a meal, but always after.
this was the same woman
who taught me to wipe from front to back, and
to watch the news hour with soft piano music playing
from the kitchen:
something about a vagus nerve.

it's the similarity of lures that determine
the difficulty of the test.
so when I remember that luscious woman can I
implode my ballooning thoughts
of skinny desirables
and cues to
not eat ?

when I think of that woman, her hips,
can I use them instead of boiling water
as the substance of beauty?

CRUMB (A LA MAMACITA)

You have no idea
what you mean to me. When I
hear your distantly-Parisian voice or
smell the English on your work clothes
it feels like how you
floated bed sheets
under *Goodnight Moon*'s eyes
then tucked them under
as if to comfortably mummify
and say
"goodnight."
Or excuse me, rather
something much less trite.
"I love you to Pluto and back.
Alright. Go to sleep. Goodnight."

And now, when we kitchen groove and
befittingly bump our hips to
"You Make My Dreams Come True,"
my heart trembles like when you
tossed me in towels
after I befriended the sand box,
and rub-a-dub-dubbed me
out of the tub.

I retain the same beating hub swirl
but now with a little boogie
and we twirl just to
spite the sink zoo
which I like to cram
with sweet batter bowls
because on Burt Street, you used to.

The little things are sinuous,
curving and turning our world.
You taught me that.
And even your little ways,
how you leave a final bite
of scone untouched,
silently whistle
to the mirror,
find a certain *je nai se quoi* about
a grocery bag with a baguette sticking out,
shine like a ruby
with uncontrollable laughter,
dart your pupils across a book,
think Hugh Jackman's a triple threat,
idolize Chinese food,
charm the elevator air,
and often let out a contented sigh,
they always scream grace
without words.
And so your grace will never be defined.
But you have no idea

Sarah Simon

what you mean to life itself, because
life's too big.
But keep with the little things.
They spell out meaning for
everyone who's watching.

LA MUJER COMO YEMA

Huelo la grasa
que se está estallando
y el blanco – a su alrededor.

Es la grasa que me hace mujer:
Tengo tatas, los senos –
estoy sana debido a la grasa.
Así pues, que me permitas comer la grasa,
la raíz de mí,
de *la vie*, porque
me permitirá llenarte,
rodearte,
estar a tu alrededor.

Oigo a la mujer,
que está gritando
y llorando
y sonriendo
y amando – a mi alrededor,
dentro de mí.

Es de la yema de la vida que puedo extender
y ser mujer

WOMAN AS YOLK

I smell the fat
that is exploding
and the white – around it.

It is fat that makes me a woman:
I have tatas, breasts –
I am healthy due to the fat.
So, let me eat the fat,
the root of me,
of *la vie*, because
it will allow me to fill you,
surround you,
be around you.

I hear the woman,
who is screaming
and crying

and smiling
and loving – around me,
inside of me.

It is from the yolk of life that I can spread
and be woman

EPOH

You ask me why I sometimes spell certain things backwards. Well, it's with *epoh* that you'll ask about it. It's with the *epoh* that you'll investigate into my peculiarities. That you'll help me find something about myself.

It's with the *epoh* that you'll help me radiate me. That you'll help me become enamored by the specific things about me. It's with the *epoh* that you'll ask *yhw*, and not just

tahw or
ohw or
woh or
gnihthton.

God forbid the *gnihthton*.

I leave little vague notes around, usually consisting of one backwards word. That's because I like to be mysterious to myself, and force myself to think, to guess, to avoid the dull. For example, I'm not going to tell you that my calendared clue *ekoarak* means "book that party," or that *eulb* means "wash your skirt," or that the dirt-accumulating word *twat* was not meant to be read backwards, because I'm really just trying to remind myself of *gnihthton* that's your business.

All these obscurities are haphazardly-sticky noted with the *epoh* that I'll remain a mystery to myself – in the little ways. And that I'll be intriguing enough to draw you in.

LIST OF CREDITS

c i n g u l u m (Gandy Dancer Issue 4.2 ; https://www.gandy-dancer.org/archives/issue-4-2/4-2-poetry/sarah-simon/)

core (Fearsome Critters, Vol. 1 ; https://www.amazon.com/Fearsome-Critters-Arts-Journal-1/dp/1717105602/)

La mujer como yema/Woman as yolk (The Journal of Latina Critical Feminism, Vol. 1, Issue 1 ; https://docs.wixstatic.com/ugd/ff2d79_bc9e56ae66454cc2b78558b6ba561f15.pdf)

ABOUT THE AUTHOR

Sarah Simon was born in New York City in 1995, when – according to her father –fireworks left over from the July 4th holiday went off nearby. Romantic, isn't it?

Whether or not it happened that way, that's how she gets her poetic inspiration: in spurts of emotion and creativity, in moments and fleeting minutes, in fireworks. She began writing poetry from a young age, finding that the medium really suited her brain: there was less of a need to connect thoughts logically, and an emphasis on honoring moments as they came.

As a young girl, she just really loved food, and, when measured against her peers, found herself "plump," overweight. Then, in her early adolescent through young adult years, she would craft and crave a ritualistic relationship with food, exercise, and her body, which would come to affect all aspects of her life and many people around her. No matter the clamoring biological need for calories and rest, her disordered eating was her obsession; it was the thing in life that she could orchestrate entirely on her own, without anyone else having a say. In fact, when others did say something, she got a high off of the *you're so skinny!* and the *everything looks good on you!* She even felt a secret firework of pride go off inside when her mother looked at her bones gravely, and when her doctor told her that she needed to eat more, as if it were easy.

But all that wasn't enough; she kept going. She kept going until when, in April 2014, she suffered from traumatic brain injury (TBI) and had to leave college. During recovery, she began practicing yoga, more deeply appreciating the love and support of the people around her, and developing a healthier relationship with food and her body. Six months later, she would return to college and go on to graduate with a B.A. in psychology in 2017. Unsure of what to do next, she traveled to Quito, Ecuador to teach English. There, she more formally solidified her interest and experience in Spanish language and culture and applied for a scholarship to as a Fulbright English Teaching Assistant (ETA) in Uruguay. From March to November 2019, she will be teaching English in the South American country, and continue writing and photographing – not to mention getting used to the vaguely-Italian accent of the *uruguayos*, as a *gringa* coming in with all the *quiteña* lingo. From what she hears, Uruguay is big on its *parrilladas*, or grilled meat – yup, she'll be eating that.

It is with great pleasure and relief that Sarah publishes this poetry collection; eating disorders should be more deeply recognized and discussed. And since they aren't so logical, she believes that poetry has a lot to add to the conversation.

www.ingramcontent.com/pod-product-compliance
Lightning Source LLC
Chambersburg PA
CBHW030121100526
44591CB00009B/482